THE
FIDDLE
LEAF
FIG
EXPERT

CLAIRE AKIN

For my mom, Nancy,

who taught me everything I know about

making a house a home.

CONTENTS

"*Don't dig up in doubt what you planted in faith.*"

INTRODUCTION

I'm Claire, and I love fiddle leaf fig plants! I'm a writer, gardener, houseplant lover, and fiddle leaf fig grower. I have an outdoor garden with twenty-one hybrid tea roses. My twenty-six houseplants include at least a dozen varieties, but my favorites are my half-dozen fiddle leaf fig plants. I wrote this guide to share what I've learned about growing healthy and vibrant fiddle leaf figs.

It drives me crazy when people tell me that fiddle leaf fig plants are hard to grow. There are certain plants that are challenging (I'm looking at you, maidenhair fern), but a *Ficus lyrata* (fiddle leaf fig) is not of one them.

Fiddle leaf fig trees are among the easiest and most rewarding plants to own. There are only a few simple things that can go wrong with them, and these are relatively easy to remedy. The plants are also resistant to pests and disease (unlike my twenty-one prize roses).

The fiddle leaf fig has become one of the most popular house plants in the world in recent years. In 2016, *The New York*

Times called fiddle leaf figs "The 'It' Plant of the Design World." They've been featured in home interior magazines, gone viral on Pinterest, and even made cameos in about a dozen Super Bowl commercials in 2018.

Yet there remains an astounding lack of information available on how to care properly for your fiddle leaf fig plant. Much of the information available on the internet is unreliable and overly simplified. Some of the information out there is just plain wrong and can harm your plant.

For fiddle leaf fig lovers who want to understand what their plant needs to thrive, to confidently diagnose problems, and to provide the best care for their plant, resources are lacking. That's why I have written this guide. It's my goal to explain everything I know about growing a gorgeous fiddle leaf fig plant without stressing. I've avoided overly scientific explanations and focused on the most helpful, clear, and actionable information.

As a writer and a fiddle leaf fig lover, I created this resource to provide helpful information so that you can feel more confident and enjoy your plant more. My aim is for this to be the only resource on fiddle leaf figs that you'll ever need. I hope it helps you and your plant!

For more information, tools, and products, visit us online at fiddleleaffigplant.com.

"Grow
through
what
you go
through."

THE BENEFITS OF YOUR FIDDLE LEAF FIG PLANT

You probably got your fiddle leaf fig plant to provide your home with greenery and beauty. So you might be surprised to learn that there are several other benefits. Taking good care of your plant may help you be happier and healthier, and even live longer!

One of the most important benefits of plants in the home is that they basically do the opposite of our respiration (breathing) process: they absorb carbon dioxide and other toxic chemicals and release pure oxygen. Research by NASA shows that houseplants can clean air better than any man-made technologies can. In fact, NASA's studies show that houseplants can remove over eighty-five percent of air toxins within a twenty-four-hour period.

Another benefit is that plants increase the relative humidity in our homes by releasing water through a process called transpiration. Greater humidity can help people who suffer from asthma and allergies. Houseplants can also lower air temperature during the summer, keeping your home more comfortable and cool. Research shows that the presence of plants can improve our health, decreasing the incidence of

fatigue, colds, headaches, coughs, sore throats, and flu-like symptoms. Placing plants in your bedroom may help you sleep better at night.

But what may be more important than keeping us healthy is how plants make us feel. People have been bringing plants into their living spaces for centuries, and new studies give us some evidence as to why.

Several experimental studies have shown that plants in hospital rooms can lead to

- lower blood pressure
- increased attentiveness
- improved well-being
- improved perceptions of the space
- lower levels of anxiety during recovery from surgery

Research shows that plants make us happier in our homes

and more satisfied at work. Plants such as fiddle leaf figs tend to make us feel more relaxed and calm. They can even increase concentration and productivity by fifteen percent.

Well-cared-for plants can outlive their human caretakers and provide a rewarding long-term relationship across multiple generations. Caring for a plant and helping it thrive can be thoroughly satisfying and can even reduce feelings of loneliness and depression. Many cultures believe that plants bring good luck and can improve our happiness. Whatever you believe, caring for a fiddle leaf fig plant can be a challenging and rewarding hobby for years to come.

"Plant lady is the new cat lady."

A Brief History of Fiddle Leaf Fig Plants

Fiddle leaf fig plants have been growing in the wild for millions of years. They're native to West African countries such as Sierra Leone, where they can grow forty to sixty feet tall and bear small green fruit.

They belong to the Moraceae family, which is the plant family of fig and mulberry trees. There are more than 1,100 plants in the large Moraceae family; fiddle leaf figs are a species of the *Ficus* genus and have about 850 sibling species.

A KILLER IN THE WILD?

You may think of the fiddle leaf fig as a docile houseplant, but in the wild, they can behave quite differently. *Ficus lyrata* is one of the banyan figs, which start life as an epiphyte (a plant that grows on another plant).

They land as a seed at the very top of another tree, where there is abundant sunlight. When the seed germinates, it grows downward toward the ground and may strangle its host plant as it competes for sunlight in the thick rainforest. Banyan fig trees include the Indian banyan, which is the national tree of India.

The fiddle leaf fig plant was named for its large violin-shaped leaves. The leaves can measure up to twelve inches wide and thirty inches long. They're thick and leathery in texture, with a beautiful dark green color.

RISE TO STARDOM

The rise of the fiddle leaf fig to popularity as a houseplant coincided with the launch of Pinterest in 2010. When Pinterest really took off, with more than ten million users in 2012, so did the fiddle leaf fig. One reason for this is that the fiddle leaf fig plant photographs so well, and Pinterest is driven by beautiful home design photography.

Ikea started carrying small fiddle leaf figs back in 2013, for the low price of $13.99, which really triggered their popularity with the masses. Today, big box stores such as Home Depot carry large fiddle leaf fig trees for about $100.

Purchasing a good plant can still be a challenge, since it's tough to transport a large specimen. The fiddle leaf fig is the number one selling plant of online houseplant retailer Leon and George, which delivers plants in Los Angeles and San Francisco. With no end to the fever in sight, the famous New York City plant store The Sill is constantly selling out of its supply.

ON THE BIG SCREEN

Fiddle leaf figs can be seen everywhere today on TV and in the movies. Plant purists will point out that they weren't popular as interior design plants until at least 2005, so it is almost certainly a set design error when you see a fiddle leaf fig in a movie that is supposed to take place before the year 2000.

In contrast, the set designers for the iconic TV show *Mad Men* were ruthlessly accurate with their plant selection. You'll often see the popular houseplants of the 1960s, including parlor palms, pothos, and large monsteras. But you won't see one fiddle leaf fig in the entire series.

WHY DO WE LOVE FIDDLE LEAF FIGS?

Why did fiddle leaf figs get so popular? In addition to the reasons mentioned above, they're the ultimate statement plant, changing the look and feel of any space they inhabit. Millennials love them because, with their bold and memorable silhouette, they're not your mother's *Ficus*.

There's also the strangely alluring quality of the large glossy leaves that makes us imagine how the world looked a million years ago. Finally, there's the fact that many people believe they're hard to grow, and we all love a challenge.

In fact, I don't think the fiddle leaf fig would have become so popular without so many people saying they're hard to grow. You'll encounter many more fiddle leaf figs online than you will in real life because so many people are intimidated by them.

Today, their popularity has soared to new heights. You can't scroll through your Pinterest feed without seeing one, and they are even available at local grocery stores in some areas. And this is no passing fad: they're likely to be around for a long time. At the end of the day, great design is timeless, and there's no better interior design plant than the fiddle leaf fig.

A Quick
Refresher on How
Plants Work

Remember in high school biology class, when you learned about photosynthesis and how plants replenish oxygen in the atmosphere? This quick refresher on the basics of plant biology will give you a better grasp on what your fiddle leaf fig needs to be happy and to thrive.

Plants live and grow by absorbing light from the sun and using chlorophyll within the leaves to turn carbon dioxide and water into energy. This process is called photosynthesis. Without light, plants simply cannot grow.

In photosynthesis plants collect and store the energy from sunlight. They absorb gases (mainly carbon dioxide) through the pores (stomata) of their leaves. Combining carbon dioxide and water, they turn the energy from the sunlight into chemical energy (sugar) and release oxygen as a byproduct. Remembering that sunlight, carbon dioxide, and water are the foundation of a plant's life can help you provide your plant with the ideal environment to thrive.

THE ANATOMY OF A PLANT

There are hundreds of thousands of varieties of plants, but most of them share the same anatomy. These are the key parts of your fiddle leaf fig.

THE ROOTS

Perhaps the most important part of the plant is the root system, which first and foremost acts as its anchor. The roots also transport water and nutrients from the soil up to the stem of your plant. Roots need both water and oxygen to live, so proper drainage is essential to keeping your plant's root system healthy.

THE STEM

The stem of your fiddle leaf fig acts as its structural support system and transports nutrients and water from the roots to the leaves. In small, young fiddle leaf fig plants, the stems may be thin and flexible, but in larger, older plants the stems become the trunk of the tree.

THE LEAVES

Your fiddle leaf fig's leaves are green because they're filled with chlorophyll. Photosynthesis takes place within the leaves, and it is the leaves that release the oxygen produced as a byproduct of this process.

Fiddle leaf fig leaves are protected by three layers of an epidermis and a thick cuticle on the surface of the plant. They have an extensive vascular system, with veins running through the leaves to transport nutrients. The stomata on the surface of the leaf constantly release water and oxygen, which can lead to a plant becoming dry if the humidity is too low.

THE FLOWERS

In the wild, fiddle leaf fig plants produce flowers to aid in reproduction. As in almost all plants, the flowers contain both the male and the female reproductive organs of the plant. Pollination within the flower leads to the production of fruit.

But fiddle leaf fig flowers don't look much like flowers at all. They're actually tiny purple leaves. Many fiddle leaf fig plants will never flower indoors. If you notice that your plant is flowering, you can be sure that it is thriving, since plants will not put their energy toward flowers unless they're in good health.

THE FRUIT

Plants produce fruit to protect and transport their seeds so that new plants can grow. Many people don't realize that fiddle leaf fig plants produce fruit in their natural outdoor habitat. Fiddle leaf fig fruits are green and look like figs. They are fleshy in texture and filled with seeds. Indoor fiddle leaf figs will almost never produce fruit.

WHAT'S REQUIRED FOR PHOTOSYNTHESIS?

We've established that photosynthesis is how plants create the energy they need to live. But what is required for photosynthesis? There are four critical components:

1. light
2. carbon dioxide
3. water
4. nutrients

Plants get the first three components from their surroundings but must get nutrients from the soil. They need seventeen important nutrients: nitrogen (chemical symbol N), phosphorus (P), potassium (K), calcium (Ca), sulfur (S), magnesium (Mg), carbon (C), oxygen (O), hydrogen (H), iron (Fe), boron (B), chlorine (Cl), manganese (Mn), zinc (Zn), copper (Cu), molybdenum (Mo), and nickel (Ni). These nutrients can be supplied by the soil or by fertilization. We'll review everything you need to know about fertilizer later.

"Be patient with yourself, nothing blooms in nature all year long."

IS YOUR PLANT HEALTHY?

You likely purchased this book because you'd like to know everything there is to know about caring properly for your fiddle leaf fig plant. But before we dive too deep, let's review the basics. If you have an urgent problem that you want to address now, this section will give you some guidance on how to take action today.

Brown spots. Dropping leaves. Slow growth. These are some of the symptoms of common ailments of fiddle leaf figs trees that can even kill your prize plant. The good news is that most of these problems are easily cured if you know what to look for. Here are six ways to tell whether your fiddle leaf fig tree is healthy and advice on where to start if it's not.

1. ARE THERE BROWN SPOTS ON THE LEAVES?

One of the most common problems with fiddle leaf fig plants is brown spots on the leaves. It might seem tricky to diagnose what's causing these spots, given that the two main causes are opposites: over- and underwatering. But it's pretty easy

to tell which sin is harming your plant if you take a closer look.

Are your brown spots starting in the middle of the leaf and spreading? This is likely caused by a fungal disorder due to overwatering. Keeping the roots too wet can lead to root rot, a fungus that will spread to the leaves and eventually kill your plant. If your plant has root rot, stop watering now, repot with proper drainage, and cut off the affected leaves.

If your plant's brown spots are starting on the edges of the leaves and spreading inward, the cause is likely dry air, drafts, and underwatering—basically a dry plant. Try to move your plant to a more humid area away from dry air or heater vents, and set a reminder to water your plant every week.

Brown spots can also be caused by leaf trauma, which is common during shipping, so if your new plant arrives with injured leaves, cut them off at the stem and wait for the plant to recover.

But it's most likely your brown spots are related to watering, so you'll want to read the watering section of this book thoroughly to learn more.

2. ARE THE NEW LEAVES SMALLER THAN THE OLDER LEAVES?

If your fiddle leaf fig plant has new growth, that's a good sign. If the newest leaves are larger than the older leaves, that's a great sign! This means that your plant is healthy enough to invest resources toward new growth.

If the new leaves are smaller than the existing leaves, it may be a sign that your plant doesn't have the right nutrients to grow well. Focus on the fundamentals of watering properly, providing adequate sunlight, and feeding your plant with liquid fertilizer.

Read the fertilizing section of this book to learn everything you need to know about properly feeding your plant.

3. IS YOUR PLANT DROPPING LEAVES?

One common and serious problem is a plant dropping its leaves. You need to act fast to save your plant before it's too late.

The causes to consider are underwatering and overwatering. How can you tell which? If the oldest leaves toward the bottom of your plant are falling off first, it's likely overwatering. If the leaves are falling off all over the plant, it's likely underwatering or too dry of an environment.

Refer to the watering section of this guide to fix your plant in a hurry.

4. ARE THE LEAVES TURNING YELLOW?

Yellow leaves on a fiddle leaf fig plant have three probable causes. The most likely is lack of sunlight, followed by poor nutrition. A third cause is an insect problem, but this is much less likely. If you suspect insects, look for small brown spots where the insects have attached to your plant and bleed the sap, causing the leaves to turn yellow and fall off.

Too little sun and too much water will cause yellowing of your plant's leaves. Let your plant dry out and make sure it's getting enough light. If you still have problems, make sure you are feeding your plant with liquid fertilizer at least every other time you water it so that it has the nutrients it needs for dark green growth.

Review the watering and feeding sections of this book to learn what you need to know.

5. DOES YOUR PLANT HAVE STUNTED GROWTH?

A healthy fiddle leaf fig tree should be putting out new leaves every four to six weeks during the growing season. Growth tends to be in spurts, in which the plant will grow two to four new leaves in a matter of a few days. In the winter, it's normal not to have any new growth.

If your plant seems to have stunted growth, that's a clue that it doesn't have the resources it needs to thrive. Make sure it gets adequate sunlight and proper watering, and invest in a good plant fertilizer to provide the nutrients it needs for new growth.

Review the fertilizer section of this guide.

6. IS YOUR PLANT DIRTY OR DUSTY?

In order to efficiently perform photosynthesis, your plant needs to absorb light and breathe in carbon dioxide through its leaves. A plant that is too dirty or dusty can have trouble breathing and absorbing light. Make sure you shower your plant every three to six months to keep it clean and healthy.

Refer to the cleaning section of this book.

◆ ◆ ◆

Once you figure out what is wrong with your fiddle leaf fig plant, it's easy to correct the problem and put your plant on the fast track back to health. Be consistent with your plant's care, and be patient while it recovers. Look for consistent new growth of large, dark green leaves as the sign of a healthy fiddle leaf fig tree.

"To plant a garden is to believe in tomorrow."

YOUR QUICK-
START GUIDE

It's not that fiddle leaf fig trees are hard to keep healthy; it's more that many fiddle leaf fig tree owners are houseplant beginners. They don't have the confidence of a houseplant veteran, and they may second-guess their decisions when caring for their new plant. Novices may water their tree too often and inadvertently cause root rot. Or they may forget about their tree completely and kill it with drought.

Over- and underwatering are the two most common killers of a fiddle leaf fig tree. As a new plant owner, the best thing you can do for your tree is master the art of watering. Once you've done that, it's helpful to learn the ten simple secrets to keep a fiddle leaf fig healthy.

THE TEN COMMANDMENTS OF FIDDLE LEAF FIG CARE

Caring for your fiddle leaf fig can seem complex and over-whelming if you are a first-time plant owner. Good care makes your plant stronger and more resistant to disease. But poor care creates a downward spiral of sickness. There are ten critical aspects to successful care. Follow these rules for a happy and healthy plant.

1. **Provide Proper Drainage.** Your plant's root system is the basis of its health. Many people are not aware that roots need both water and oxygen to work properly. Adequate drainage allows your plant's root system to breathe and stay healthy. Without it, root rot can set in and kill your plant.

2. **Don't Drown Your Plant.** It's important to let your plant's soil dry out a bit between waterings. Overwatering is one of the most common mistakes fiddle leaf fig owners make. Be aware of your plant's water requirements, and make sure you aren't drowning it.

3. **Give Your Plant a Rest in Winter.** During the winter, your plant receives less sun, so it has less energy to complete its metabolic functions. As a result, it uses less water and nutrients. Water less and suspend fertilization during the winter to give your plant a chance to rest.

4. **Accept the Loss of Older Leaves.** Plants are always shedding older leaves in favor of new growth. Fiddle leaf fig plants drop their lower leaves as they grow taller. Don't worry if your plant regularly drops its lower leaves, so long as it has healthy new growth.

5. **Give Your Plant Humidity.** The ideal humidity for a fiddle leaf fig is between thirty and sixty-five percent. If you live in a very dry climate, you may need to provide your plant with extra humidity by misting it or using a humidifier. Be sure not to put your fiddle leaf fig near a heater vent, which will dry it out.

6. **Treat Problems Immediately.** Fiddle leaf fig plants are relatively slow growers, since their large leaves require a lot of energy to build. This makes treating ailments quickly even more important, because it takes them so long to recover from problems. Be sure to act fast if you see brown spots, leaf drop, or an insect infestation.

7. **Repot When Needed.** If your fiddle leaf fig is healthy, its root system will begin to outgrow its pot in a few years. When you see roots growing near the bottom or edges of the pot, it may be time to repot to give your plant more space to grow. If you've reached your maximum container size, you can top-dress instead of repotting: remove the top four inches of soil and replace it with new soil.

8. **Feed Your Plant Properly.** Fiddle leaf fig plants require a lot of nutrients to grow their large leaves. Feed them with a liquid fertilizer such as Fiddle Leaf Fig Plant Food, which is specially formulated with a nitrogen-phosphorus-potassium (N-P-K) ratio of 3-1-2. (See the section on feeding your plant for an explanation of this term.)

9. **Use the Correct Tools.** It's important to have the proper tools to take care of your plant, including a watering can, moisture meter, sharp pruning shears, and even a rolling plant stand that allows you to move and rotate your fiddle leaf fig.

10. **Check on Your Plant Every Week.** The best way to take good care of your plant is to get to know it better. Take the time to check on your fiddle leaf fig every week. First, check whether the soil is wet or dry before you water. Look at the leaves for any signs of wilting or brown spots. Rotate your plant to make sure it gets even sunlight. Finally, make an overall assessment of your plant and note any changes such as new growth.

THE TEN COMMANDMENTS OF FIDDLE LEAF FIG CARE

1. *Provide Proper Drainage.*
2. *Don't Drown Your Plant.*
3. *Give Your Plant a Rest in Winter.*
4. *Accept the Loss of Older Leaves.*
5. *Give Your Plant Humidity.*
6. *Treat Problems Immediately.*
7. *Repot When Needed.*
8. *Feed Your Plant Properly.*
9. *Use the Correct Tools.*
10. *Check on Your Plant Every Week.*

"You can't buy happiness, but you can buy plants, and that's pretty much the same thing."

WHERE TO BUY A FIDDLE LEAF FIG PLANT

If you're ready to make the investment in a fiddle leaf fig tree, you'll want to spend some time researching your options and choosing the best plant for you. Which plant you buy is important, not least since *Ficus lyrata* can live longer than you do. Many options are available, depending on how large of a plant you're looking for. Here's where to buy a fiddle leaf fig tree.

1. HOME DEPOT OR LOWE'S

Check your local home store's indoor houseplant section for great deals on a fiddle leaf fig plant. Smaller plants under three feet are often priced at around $25, which isn't a steal but is a fair price for a healthy plant. You'll often find excellent deals on large fiddle leaf fig trees here. I once purchased a six-foot-tall tree for $99, which would have cost at least $200 in a plant nursery.

Keep in mind you'll need to transport the plant home, which can be a real challenge if you're buying a larger plant. Mine suffered minor damage lying on its side in my small SUV. Be sure to repot your new plant as soon as you get it home. Some stores sell notoriously dry plastic pots that need to be watered every single day until you repot.

2. IKEA

IKEA often has sales on small fiddle leaf fig plants, at prices from $12 to $15. You won't find a giant tree here, but for a starter plant, you can't beat the price. Choose the healthiest plant you can find and expect to spend a few years watching it grow.

3. A PLANT NURSERY

For larger plants with guaranteed health, a plant nursery is the place to go. Expect to pay more ($200–300) for a six-foot-tall tree, but this is where you'll typically find higher-quality plants raised by experts. Call first, because not all nurseries have fiddle leaf fig trees in stock.

4. ONLINE

You can find a variety of fiddle leaf fig trees online through the websites of Home Depot and plant nurseries, and even on Amazon.com, but expect to pay a little more and plan for the additional shipping cost. The downside to purchasing online is you're typically buying a smaller plant, and it may suffer damage from the dry air and cold during shipping.

A three- to four-foot-tall plant can run $150 plus shipping online, and you'll have to repot it once it arrives. However, if you can't find a good plant locally, buying online is the way to go.

5. LÉON & GEORGE

If you're in San Francisco or Los Angeles, you can buy a fiddle leaf fig tree that comes with free delivery, a thirty-day guarantee, and expert plant care support from Léon & George, an upscale plant service that helps connect people and nature. Fiddle leaf fig trees start at $299, including the pot.

"Someone is sitting in the shade today because someone planted a tree a long time ago."

WHAT ELSE TO CONSIDER

Once you find your dream fiddle leaf fig, you'll need to re-pot it in a good pot, with high-quality indoor potting soil, and create the perfect drainage situation. Read on to learn more.

CREATING PERFECT DRAINAGE

Buying a container with good drainage may be the most important investment you make in the health of your fiddle leaf fig. No soil or fertilizer can correct problems caused by poor drainage. It's important to get your drainage right to set your plant up for success; without proper drainage, the roots cannot be healthy, and the vitality of your plant will suffer.

Fiddle leaf fig plants prefer fast-draining soil and containers so that their roots can stay evenly moist and never become wet and soggy. Perfect drainage allows you to fully water the plant in such a way that the root ball is completely saturated and excess water runs out the drainage holes. This way, there is no risk of soggy soil and root rot.

Your container should have drainage holes that allow excess water to escape the soil. Never attempt to grow a fiddle leaf fig in a container without drainage holes. My favorite type of pot for a fiddle leaf fig is one with a large drainage hole at the bottom edge of the container, which allows the water to escape without any loss of soil.

One way to reduce the likelihood of losing soil each time you water is to place a layer of gravel in the bottom of your container before you add the soil. Another option is to use a coffee filter over the drainage holes.

If you have a decorative container without a drainage hole, double-potting allows you to provide your plant with proper drainage *and* enjoy your decorative container. Place a well-draining container within your decorative pot and check the drainage each week to make sure your plant can drain properly.

CHOOSING THE BEST SOIL

After drainage, the soil you choose may be the next most important decision you make for the health of your fiddle leaf fig plant. Fast-draining, well-aerated soils are the best choice for a fiddle leaf fig, which prefers relatively dry soil to keep its roots moist but not wet.

Soil for indoor plants performs four basic functions:

1. anchoring the roots to provide support to the plant
2. providing nutrients for growth and photosynthesis
3. allowing oxygen to reach the root system
4. delivering ample water to the roots

A versatile soil designed for houseplants should perform all four of these functions well. Be sure to choose a fast-draining soil when possible to reduce the risk of root rot. Most houseplant soil blends combine perlite to speed drainage and peat moss to retain moisture. Any good houseplant soil mix will work for your fiddle leaf fig.

MiracleGro indoor potting mix is specifically designed to provide aeration, fast drainage, and nutrition for your plants, while being resistant to fungus and gnats. Keep in mind that soil will provide nutrition for your fiddle leaf fig only for the first three to six months; after that, you need to fertilize your plant to make sure it gets adequate nutrition.

CHOOSING A CONTAINER FOR YOUR FIDDLE LEAF FIG TREE

Adding a gorgeous fiddle leaf fig tree to your home is a fantastic way to make a statement and wow your guests. But the plant itself provides only half the impact. A stunning container for your fiddle leaf fig tree will bring focus to your plant and provide an amazing aesthetic for your home.

SIZE AND COLOR

Believe it or not, there are actually "rules" for choosing a pot for your houseplant, at least according to D. G. Hessayon, the author of *The Houseplant Expert*, the world's best-selling book on growing houseplants.

Hessayon argues that your container should provide balance to the overall size of the plant. A small plant in a huge pot looks silly and will have drainage problems. A very large plant in too small of a pot may be unstable and won't have the proper visual proportions.

Hessayon also argues that your container should not clash with the color and texture of your plant. If you have a brightly colored or variegated plant, you should use a solid or plain container. For flowering plants, you shouldn't use a patterned pot that competes with the flowers for attention. Lucky for us, fiddle leaf fig plants have a solid color and smooth texture, so we can get away with using really eye-catching pots.

BE SURE TO MEASURE

Especially if you are ordering your decorative container online, measure your plant's current container to be sure that it will fit comfortably inside. Measure the diameter across the top and bottom of your current container; then measure its height. Choose your new container to be at least two inches wider in diameter at the top and bottom and four to six inches taller so that it hides your functional container.

THE MOST BEAUTIFUL POTS FOR A FIDDLE LEAF FIG TREE

Finding the perfect pot for your fiddle leaf fig tree may take some searching. Plant nurseries often have a great selection, and you can even find decorative pots at discount stores such as Home Goods or Ross. But for those of us who like to buy online, here are my favorite pots on Amazon. Unless otherwise noted, they provide proper drainage.

WOVEN SEAGRASS BASKET

This beautiful woven seagrass basket provides the perfect home for your fiddle leaf fig. It comes in small, medium, and large to fit a variety of plant sizes. It's hand woven with sustainably grown seagrass and gives a natural, peaceful look to your home.[1]

WHITE CERAMIC PLANTER WITH WOODEN STAND

These understated white ceramic planters with wooden stands originally appeared on the pages of Crate & Barrel catalogs and have become popular on Pinterest. They provide an elevated focal point for your plant, without distracting attention from its natural beauty. These planters are perfect

---

1 Check the price on Amazon here: https://www.amazon.com/ DUFMOD-Natural-Seagrass-Storage-Laundry/dp/B01I5QNZZM.

Woven seagrass basket

*Ceramic planter
with wooden stand*

*Blue-and-white
ceramic pot*

*Sparkling white
pot for a large tree*

Ocean blue

*Stunning
in silver*

for small to medium-sized fiddle leaf fig plants; avoid using them for a very large plant since they could be top heavy.[2]

BLUE-AND-WHITE CERAMIC POT
One of the most common questions I get asked on my blog is where I bought the gorgeous blue-and-white pot for my fiddle leaf fig Goose. I purchased it at a local plant nursery, but you can find a similar product online. Something about the simple blue-and-white pattern turns your fiddle leaf fig into an interesting work of art. This Moroccan pot is only eight inches tall, but it is perfect for a smaller fiddle leaf fig.[3]

SPARKLING WHITE POT FOR A LARGE TREE
It's tough to find pots large enough for a full-size fiddle leaf fig tree. This large planter measures seventeen inches in diameter. Because it's made of fiberglass, it's not as heavy as a ceramic pot. There are no drainage holes, so make sure you use this only as a decorative container.[4]

OCEAN BLUE
This large and inexpensive pot measures fifteen inches in diameter and is twelve inches tall. It's perfect for a home with ocean-themed decor or a cool color palette. A great budget

---

2 Check the price on Amazon here: https://www.amazon.com/Case-Study-Ceramic-Planter-Wood/dp/B00KYY1J5C.

3 Check the price on Amazon here: https://www.amazon.com/Moroccan-Spanish-Ceramic-Planter-Handmade/dp/B017MPC7S8.

4 Check the price on Amazon here: https://www.amazon.com/Shiny-White-Round-Fiberglass-Planter/dp/B07C58ZNNQ.

option, this plastic container is designed to look ceramic at a fraction of the cost and weight.[5]

STUNNING IN SILVER

I absolutely adore this set of aluminum silver planters and have a set for my fiddle leaf fig Bruiser in my office. The set comes with three pots, with the largest being sixteen inches in diameter and twenty-one inches tall. You could use the other two for accompanying houseplants to create a grouped focal display. There are no drainage holes, so you'll want to use these as decorative containers for your existing pot.[6]

PROTECTING YOUR FLOORS AND SURFACES

No matter which planter you choose, be sure to protect your floors and surfaces by adding self-adhesive felt pads to the underside of the container.[7] This allows for some airflow below your plant and protects your surfaces from scratches. If you have a very large fiddle leaf fig, a plant caddy makes it easy to move and turn your plant.[8]

---

5   Check the price on Amazon here: https://www.amazon.com/GARDENGOODZ-Honeysuckle-Planter-Patio-Pot/dp/B07B5HT7J2.

6   Check the price on Amazon here: https://www.amazon.com/Piece-Round-Pot-Planter-Set/dp/B01JJ6D0A2.

7   See https://www.amazon.com/Self-Stick-Furniture-Round-Felt-Surfaces/dp/B001WAK5X4.

8   See https://www.amazon.com/Plant-Stand-18410-Under-16-Inch/dp/B001F5UY3M.

"Wherever life plants you, grow with grace."

How to Repot a Fiddle Leaf Fig Plant

When you're getting ready to repot a fiddle leaf fig tree, you may feel overwhelmed because of the size of the root ball or the apparent delicateness of the plant. Many people will tell you that repotting a fiddle leaf fig is complex or difficult, but it's actually easy to do and does not present a big risk to the plant. In fact, especially if you're repotting a plant you've just bought, your fiddle leaf fig will be much happier in its new pot, so don't delay. Here's the easiest way to repot a fiddle leaf fig tree.

GETTING READY TO REPOT A FIDDLE LEAF FIG TREE

1. DON'T WAIT TO REPOT YOUR NEW PLANT

If you purchased your plant from Home Depot or another wholesaler, it probably came in a plastic growing pot. These containers have drainage holes on the side that are designed to keep the roots dry as a bone. That's because the growers water their plants daily to soak the roots, and the growing pots are designed to drain immediately. This reduces the risk of root rot, but it's dangerous for your plant once you get it home.

Fiddle leaf figs can dry out and suffer permanent damage within just a few days in these pots, so don't wait to repot your plant. If you must wait, water your plant every single day while it's in the grower's pot. Make sure you pour the water onto the plant slowly so that it has a chance to sink in and doesn't just run out the side drainage holes.

2. UNDERSTAND PROPER DRAINAGE

The most important long-term investment you can make in your fiddle leaf fig plant's health is to learn about proper drainage. Fiddle leaf fig trees are susceptible to root rot, so you'll want to make sure your container has perfect drainage and that your plant will never sit in water. This means using a container with holes, with an optional ballast-like gravel or similar materials at the bottom of the container to keep the root ball dry.

3. SELECT THE RIGHT CONTAINER

You'll need to get a container that is three to four inches larger in diameter across the top than your plant's current container. Grab a tape measure to make sure your new container is both wider and at least four inches taller than your existing container. Don't go too big, as pots that are too large can promote root rot. At most, the new pot should

be six inches larger in diameter than the current pot. Most large fiddle leaf fig trees at Home Depot are in twelve- or fourteen-inch containers, so a sixteen- or eighteen-inch pot will work.

Your new pot will need holes at the bottom for drainage or it's plant homicide. I recommend a ceramic pot with a drainage hole and reservoir basin to avoid dripping. These are available at most nurseries and big box stores.

4. GET THE RIGHT POTTING SOIL

It is important to choose a soil that provides your plant with nutrients and allows for good drainage and moisture control. I like to use Nature's Care potting mix, which is about $9 for a large bag at Home Depot. You will definitely have soil left over, so you may want to get two smaller bags ($4 each) if you don't want to store the extra soil. Do not be tempted to use dirt from your yard or soil for succulents or other plants. Houseplants need soil designed to provide air circulation and water retention. Any good houseplant or potting soil will do the trick.

REPOTTING A FIDDLE LEAF FIG TREE

Now that you've prepared your materials, it's time to repot your plant. It's best to do these steps outside, as they'll get a bit messy. If going outside isn't an option, put down an old bed sheet to capture the excess dirt.

1. FILL THE NEW CONTAINER WITH FOUR INCHES OF SOIL

If you'd like to add gravel to the bottom of your pot to improve drainage, now is the time. Use a one-inch layer of gravel at the very bottom of your pot. Then, add a four-inch layer of soil to your new container to provide a bed for the root ball to rest on. Make sure your root ball will not sit too high once it's in place: the top of the soil should be slightly lower than the top of the container. Add more soil if it's sitting too low.

2. Remove the Plant from the Old Container

As you remove your plant from its existing pot, be careful not to damage the roots. If the root ball is stuck, you can cut down the side of the container with scissors. I recommend not watering your plant before you repot, as watering can cause the root ball to be messier and more likely to break apart.

3. Place the Plant in the New Container and Fill with Soil

Holding the plant upright, put handfuls of soil around the base to fill in the sides of the container around the root ball. Gently compact the soil and then add more until your container is full. Don't over-compact, as your plant needs room for the roots to grow.

4. Water Your Plant Generously

Flood the pot to make sure any large air bubbles are filled in with soil. You may need to add more soil at this point if the edges of your soil are now lower than the middle. Once you've watered your plant and the soil is even across the top of the container, you're almost done; just give the leaves of the plant and the container a quick rinse to remove any dust or dirt.

5. Let Your Plant Dry and Drain the Reservoir

Give your plant an hour or so to dry off; then you'll need to drain the reservoir of the pot by tilting it sideways. To avoid leaks, make sure you've drained as much of the water in the reservoir as possible before bringing your plant inside.

6. Wait One Month, Then Fertilize

Give your plant one month to rest and recover from the transition. Then begin feeding it every time you water with Fiddle Leaf Fig Plant Food.[9] Dilute to one teaspoon per cup of water and water normally. Soon your plant will be growing new leaves and thriving!

---

9 See http://fiddleleaffigplant.com/best-fertilizer-for-a-fiddle-leaf-fig-plant/

REPOTTING A FIDDLE
LEAF FIG TREE

1. Fill the New Container with Four Inches of Soil

2. Remove the Plant from the Old Container

3. Place the Plant in the New Container and Fill with Soil

4. Water Your Plant Generously

5. Let Your Plant Dry and Drain the Reservoir

6. Wait One Month, Then Fertilize

WHERE TO PLACE YOUR FIDDLE LEAF FIG PLANT

Among the most important choices you can make for the health of your fiddle leaf fig plant is where you place it within your home. Your plant needs plenty of sunlight, but not too much strong sunlight on its leaves. Without enough sun, it will grow slowly, it will be susceptible to illness, and it could drop its leaves.

FIDDLE LEAF FIG PLANTS LOVE SUNLIGHT

When considering how much light to give your fiddle leaf fig plant, remember that they grow in the wild in Africa, where they get tons of light each day. Choose a location next to a large window where your plant will get plenty of light.

You can actually grow a fiddle leaf fig plant outside in full sun in temperate areas such as San Diego. At the San Diego Zoo, there is a sixty foot tall fiddle leaf fig thriving outdoors.

Many fiddle leaf fig owners choose a location based on the design of their home, the position of their furniture, or where they have an empty space. But considering the direction of the sun and how much light your plant will get is important when deciding where to put your fiddle leaf fig.

If you're not sure which direction your home faces, use your phone's compass app to see which windows face north, south, east, and west. If you're in North America, the following diagram describes the pros and cons of each direction in your home.

North-facing windows often have the least amount of total sunlight and may not provide enough sun for your fiddle leaf fig. This insufficiency is more pronounced the farther you live from the Equator. However, if you are in the southern United States, there may be enough light with a large north-facing window. Consider the size of your window and your location relative to the Equator. I have a very healthy

Where Should You Place Your Fiddle Leaf Fig Plant?

NORTH
Minimal sun, but a good possibility if you live in the Southern United States and have a large window.

WEST
Intense afternoon heat may burn leaves and dry out your plant.

EAST
Early morning sun, but likely not enough hours of sunlight to sustain a fiddle leaf fig well.

SOUTH
Best location for all day sunlight and not too much strong afternoon sun.

fiddle leaf fig plant that lives next to a north-facing sliding glass door here in San Diego.

East-facing windows have plenty of early-morning sun but little to no afternoon sun, when the rays are stronger. Your fiddle leaf fig needs not only bright sunlight but also more than six hours of cumulative sunlight each day. Because an east-facing window may get fewer than six hours of gentle sunlight, you may be better off placing your plant in a window with more hours of stronger sun.

West-facing windows get intense afternoon sunlight, when the sun's rays are at their hottest. This puts your fiddle leaf fig at risk of burning. If you do place your plant in a west-facing window, take care it doesn't get too much direct sunlight on its leaves. If you have an overhang on the outside of your window, your plant may be better protected. If not, you may want to pull your plant back a few feet from the window so that it doesn't get direct sun.

South-facing windows get the longest duration of bright sunlight, so they make the ideal home for a fiddle leaf fig plant. Facing south, your plant will likely get more than eight hours per day of bright sun, but few direct harsh rays on its leaves.

In general, the more sunlight you can give your plant, the better. Fiddle leaf fig plants can do pretty well with moderate sunlight as well, but then the rest of their care becomes more important. Water carefully, fertilize, and rotate your plant once a week to make sure all of the leaves get access to light.

THE IDEAL TEMPERATURE FOR YOUR FIDDLE LEAF FIG

The ideal temperature for fiddle leaf fig plants is between sixty and seventy-five degrees Fahrenheit, but they can tolerate both warmer and cooler temperatures temporarily. If you are comfortable in your home, your plant will likely be too. Avoid putting your plant near a heating or cooling vent, as they do not like drafts and will suffer from lack of humidity. Likewise, don't put your plant too close to a cold window during the winter, especially if you have a draft.

HUMIDITY AND YOUR FIDDLE LEAF FIG

Fiddle leaf figs prefer more humidity if possible, but they can flourish in conditions between thirty and sixty-five percent humidity. Even in dry areas such as San Diego, fiddle leaf fig plants can thrive in normal room conditions without additional humidity.

However, if humidity drops during the winter due to running a heater, you may need to protect your fiddle leaf fig by misting it every few days to increase humidity. Start by keeping your plant away from heater vents and give it time to adjust to the dry conditions. Grouping your fiddle leaf fig with other plants can help keep relative humidity up during the winter months.

"The grass is greener where you water it."

WATERING YOUR FIDDLE LEAF FIG PLANT

Understanding how to water your fiddle leaf fig plant correctly can seem daunting. You've probably heard that fiddle leaf figs are hard to grow or finicky, which in large part is due to their specific watering requirements. If you water your plant too much (which is pretty common), you will kill it. If you don't water enough, it will suffer. What's a plant owner to do?

THE DIFFERENCE BETWEEN A DRY AND AN OVERWATERED FIDDLE LEAF FIG PLANT

The two most common problems for fiddle leaf fig plants are exact opposites: too much and too little water. Overwatering leads to root rot, a fungal condition that kills the plant's roots and leaves. Underwatering leads to a dry plant with leaf damage.

The amount of sunlight also plays a role here. Overwatering and lack of sunlight work together to produce root rot, so if your fiddle leaf fig doesn't get enough sun (and they like lots of light), its symptoms may mimic those of overwatering. Underwatering and too much sun work together to dry out and burn your plant, so you'll want to treat both issues together.

At first look, brown spots, dropping leaves, and curled leaf edges can be a symptom of both overwatering and underwatering. So how do you tell for sure whether your plant is too wet or too dry? Here are the subtle differences between an overwatered and an underwatered fiddle leaf fig plant.

Symptoms of a Dry Fiddle Leaf Fig Plant

Chronically dry plants will always have brown spots and curled leaves. Look at this extreme example of leaf curling in a plant that was completely dried out beyond repair.

The brown spots of a dry plant typically start at the edge of the leaf, not in the middle as they do with overwatering. They affect leaves all over the plant, from top to bottom, whereas root rot usually affects the lower leaves more than the top leaves. Dry plants also drop leaves throughout the plant, not just the bottom leaves. Finally, the leaves of a dry fiddle leaf fig may look otherwise healthy, whereas the leaves of a plant with root rot will begin to look sickly or yellow, or to have tiny brown spots.

Symptoms of Root Rot in a Fiddle Leaf Fig Plant

The telltale sign of too much water and not enough sunlight is that your plant will start to get brown spots in the middle of the leaf as well as at the edges. You may also see a yellowing of the leaves before they fall off. Yellow almost always means too much water and not enough sun or fertilizer.

A plant's instinct is to protect the newest growth (which has access to more sunlight in the wild) and drop the older leaves that it doesn't need as much. So a plant with root rot will drop its lowest leaves first. This image shows a plant with root rot that has lost many of its lower leaves.

HOW TO TELL IF YOUR PLANT IS GETTING TOO MUCH OR TOO LITTLE WATER

If you're confused about whether your plant has been getting too much or too little water, there are some surefire ways to tell.

Ask yourself the following questions to determine whether you are overwatering:

1. **Do you water more than once a week?** If so, your plant is probably overwatered.
2. **Is the soil wet to the touch one inch below the surface?** Stick your finger in and find out. If so, overwatering is likely.
3. **Do your plant's leaves have very dark brown or black spots or edges?** This could signify too much water.
4. **Are there flies in your plant's soil or does it smell musty?** Too much water is the culprit.

Here are some ways to tell whether you've been underwatering your plant:

1. **Are the newest leaves smaller than the existing leaves?** They may be lacking water or nutrients for growth.
2. **Is your plant dropping leaves?** This can be caused by low humidity or thirst.
3. **Does your plant have yellow leaves?** This is a sign of underwatering.
4. **Is the top inch of soil very dry?** Your plant may be thirsty.

5. **Has the soil pulled away from the pot?** This means your plant has gotten too dry in the past.

If you're still not sure whether you're over- or underwatering your plant after asking yourself these questions, you are probably overwatering. Plant owners who worry about their plants a lot tend to overwater. If you're reading this book, you obviously care about your plant, so you are more likely watering too much than too little. However, there's one thing that's even worse than under- or overwatering, and that is erratic watering.

◆ ◆ ◆

At first glance, it may be tough to determine whether you are giving your plant too much or too little water, but the things to look out for to diagnose root rot are yellowing leaves, brown spots in the middle of the leaf, and dropping of the lowest leaves. If you're still not sure, try using a moisture meter to check the water level in the soil.

WHAT IS ERRATIC WATERING?

In a sense, erratic watering is both under- and overwatering your plant. First, you may water too much for a few weeks, which can damage your plant. Then, realizing your error, you may want to let your plant's roots dry out, so you go a few weeks without watering at all. This does serious damage to your plant and can cause soil shrinkage, where the soil pulls away from the sides of the pot. This is a big problem, because the next time you water, the water runs down the sides, between the soil and the pot, and doesn't actually get to the roots of your plant.

This vicious cycle can lead to the death of your plant. The solution is to remove all of the leaves damaged by root rot (you can leave mildly damaged, dry leaves) and then set a schedule of watering your plant only once a week. Water until ten to fifteen percent of the water comes out of your pot's

drainage holes. Wait a full week and check to make sure the top inch of soil is dry before you water again.

The best thing you can do for your plant's health is to water like clockwork from the beginning and never let it dry out completely to the point that you see soil shrinkage.

HOW OFTEN SHOULD YOU WATER YOUR FIDDLE LEAF FIG?

The good news is that there's a foolproof way to water your plant just the right amount: fiddle leaf fig plants only need to be watered once a week. Set a calendar reminder. I prefer to water my plants on Friday.

Stick with your once-a-week schedule and your plant will get used to these conditions and really thrive. The best part about watering once a week is that it will give you confidence you're not over- or underwatering your plant, so you don't have to second-guess yourself or worry.

HOW MUCH SHOULD YOU WATER YOUR FIDDLE LEAF FIG?

You don't need to drench your plant to give it enough water. To keep things simple, water your plant the same amount each week. A good rule of thumb is to water until 10% of the water drains from the bottom of the container.

If you need more help, here are some additional guidelines. For plants that measure less than two feet from the soil to the tallest leaves, water with one cup each week. For plants that are two to three feet tall, water with two cups of water each week. If your plant is between three and six feet tall, use three cups of water. More than six feet tall? Water with four cups of water each week or until your container just begins to drain.

Never let your plant sit in water, and make sure your container fully drains each time you water. If the soil has pulled back from the sides of the pot in the past and the water is running out the bottom of the pot without saturating the root ball, you'll need to repot.

USING A MOISTURE METER TO KNOW WHEN TO WATER YOUR FIDDLE LEAF FIG

For fiddle leaf fig owners who want to be totally confident in watering their plant, a moisture meter is a fantastic tool. Soil moisture meters estimate the water content of soil using electrical resistance. They're cheap and easy to use, and they don't even need a battery. You can get a moisture meter only, or you can get a three-in-one moisture, pH, and light meter, which can be helpful to rule out other issues with your fiddle leaf fig. Either type of meter will cost less than $10 at Home Depot or on Amazon.

Use your moisture meter each week before you water. Make sure it's clean and don't leave it in the soil between readings, as this can damage it. After you take the reading, clean your meter and put it in a safe place.

Your moisture meter will have a gauge that shows the water content on a scale of one to ten, with ten being "wet." It may even come with a handy guide that lists the names of many common houseplants and the point at which you should

water each. Don't take this information at face value: most moisture meter manufacturers list fiddle leaf fig (*Ficus lyrata*) at a one, meaning you should let the plant completely dry out between waterings, but I find that this would take weeks for my plants and leave them damaged from lack of water.

WHERE TO TAKE YOUR READING

Of course, it matters a great deal *where* you take the reading. You can see that if you take a reading at the top two inches of the soil, it will read dry. If you stick the probe halfway down, it reads moist. All the way at the bottom, it reads wet. This is the nature of gravity and water.

Your readings will also differ if you measure close to the center of the plant, where the soil is wetter, or toward the outside of the container, where soil tends to be dryer.

So where is the right place to take an accurate reading? I recommend measuring halfway between the center of your plant and the container, and halfway between the top and bottom of your soil. Be sure to take your reading at the same place each time for consistency.

A Word of Caution about Fiddle Leaf Fig Plants from Home Depot

Pay attention to your plant's root ball here. Some plants from Home Depot have very dense root balls that do not integrate well with the surrounding soil. Even if the surrounding soil is moist, your plant's root ball may be bone dry and your plant may be dying of thirst. If your plant has a very compact root ball, take the measurement inside the edge of the root ball so that you're measuring the moisture content of the soil that actually has contact with the roots.

As I suggested above, stick the probe halfway between the center of the plant and the edge of the container, then go halfway down the soil. This will give you a consistent moisture reading at a point where most of the important roots of your plant are below the probe. I recommend waiting until your plant's soil is at a moisture level of three to four at this location (just between moist and dry) before you water.

WATER COMPLETELY, THEN LET THE SOIL DRY OUT AGAIN

The *way* you water in conjunction with using a moisture meter is important. The purpose is not to water a little bit every day to keep your plant at a moisture reading of four, since this would risk root rot and your plant's roots would never get a deep watering.

Fully water your plant so that five to ten percent of the water comes out of the drainage holes to make sure all of the soil gets wet and the roots get a good soak. Then wait a week or more for your plant to dry out again.

MONITOR THE MOISTURE LEVEL TO LEARN MORE ABOUT YOUR PLANT

It can be helpful to take a moisture reading a few days after you water to understand how your fiddle leaf fig is using its water supply. Large plants use more water, but large containers retain more water, so how fast your fiddle leaf fig uses water depends on both the size of your container and the size of your plant. Of course, dry environments and more sunlight cause your plant to use water more quickly, and fiddle leaf figs use more water in summer, when there is more light.

"Don't judge each day by the harvest you reap, but by the seeds that you plant."

FEEDING YOUR FIDDLE LEAF FIG PLANT

One common mistake people make when caring for a fiddle leaf fig is not fertilizing their plant. Unlike plants growing outdoors in the wild, where nutrients are naturally replenished in the soil and roots can search deeper for more nutrition, potted fiddle leaf figs depend on their potting soil for all nutrients.

Fiddle leaf fig plants need fertilizer for proper growth because their leaves are large and dense. If you haven't repotted your plant in over a year, chances are that your fiddle leaf fig is in desperate need of fertilizer.

WHEN TO FERTILIZE YOUR FIDDLE LEAF FIG

You should fertilize your plant every time you water, except during the winter months, when the plant will go dormant and rest. While it's not actively growing, it will not need additional nutrients.

If you live in a place with severe winters where the days get very short, fiddle leaf fig plants will stay dormant longer. In locations with mild winters, your plant may stay dormant only for a month or two before it resumes growth. This indoor fiddle leaf fig plant in sunny San Diego, California, only stopped new growth in November and started growing large healthy leaves again in early January.

As soon as the days begin getting longer and you see signs of new growth, resume fertilizing your plant with diluted plant food every time you water.

WHAT TYPE OF FERTILIZER IS BEST FOR FIDDLE LEAF FIG PLANTS?

I find that the safest and easiest type of fertilizer to use is a good liquid fertilizer. Dilute the fertilizer according to the instructions on the package to avoid overfeeding your plant, and feed up to every time you water during the growing season (not during the winter).

Plant fertilizers are categorized by their N-P-K ratio, which indicates the percentages of nitrogen, phosphorus, and potassium they contain. A 10-10-10 fertilizer, for example, contains ten percent nitrogen, ten percent phosphorus, and ten percent potassium.

The best NPK ratio for a fiddle leaf fig plant is 3-1-2. This formulation allows the plant to sustain its existing leaves and grow new ones. Because this formula is focused on growth, feed only during the growing season (not in winter) so that you do not overstimulate your plant when it's dormant. During the winter, simply water normally and skip the fertilizer.

Any liquid plant food with an NPK ratio close to 3-1-2 will work for your fiddle leaf fig. You can also purchase Fiddle Leaf Fig Plant Food, which is specially formulated for fiddle leaf figs and comes with instructions on how to properly feed your plant so that it can thrive.

"Plant dreams,
pull weeds,
and grow a
happy life."

CLEANING YOUR FIDDLE LEAF FIG PLANT

If you've had your fiddle leaf fig tree for less than a year, you may not have needed to clean the leaves yet. But if you've had it more than a year, your plant is likely suffocating with dirt and dust. To keep it alive and well, you need to clean the leaves to remove any dust.

WHY DO YOU NEED TO CLEAN YOUR FIDDLE LEAF FIG LEAVES?

Photosynthesis, folks. Fiddle leaf fig trees consume light and carbon dioxide to live, and when their leaves are covered in dust, they can't get enough of either. The plant's leaves act not only as its skin but also as its lungs, so it's critical that you keep them clean. Over time, if your tree is covered in dust, it will stop growing and eventually die.

THE BEST WAY TO CLEAN YOUR FIDDLE LEAF FIG LEAVES

There are three common methods for cleaning fiddle leaf fig tree leaves. The best method for you will depend on where you live, the size of your plant, and your access to the outdoors.

1. TAKE YOUR PLANT OUTSIDE AND SPRAY IT OFF WITH A HOSE

My favorite method of cleaning a fiddle leaf fig tree is to take it outside and spray it off with the hose. Give it a really good soak to remove all of the dust and residue. Then leave it outside for an hour or two to let it dry. Just make sure you don't leave it in direct sunlight or forget about it overnight.

Challenges of this method: If your plant is very large or heavy, it might be impossible to get it outside safely. It's helpful to keep a large fiddle leaf fig on a rolling stand so that you can roll it outside. Of course, you may not have access to an outdoor area and hose. Or you may live in a place that's too cold for this method to make sense.

2. PUT YOUR PLANT IN THE SHOWER AND SPRAY IT OFF

The second-easiest method of cleaning your fiddle leaf fig is to put it in the shower and spray it off. First, remove any decorative containers. Be sure to use room temperature water—not too hot or too cold. You may need to rotate your tree in the shower and slightly bend the plant sideways to reach the lowest leaves.

Once your plant is clean, allow it to drain for several hours.

Be aware that your plant will be heavier after its shower since the soil will be well soaked, so you may need to wait until it dries out a bit to move it back to its home.

Cons of this method: If you have a water softener, avoid fully soaking your plant's soil, since the salt from the softener can damage your plant. It may be tough to get your plant in and out of the shower, depending on the size of both. Finally, you'll want to have a towel handy to wipe up any overspray after you shower your plant.

3. Wipe the Leaves with Water and a Soft Cloth

If your plant is too large to take outside or put in the shower, your best bet may be to spray the leaves and wipe them down with water and a soft cloth. It's not good for your plant to put anything other than plain water on the leaves, so avoid the temptation to use any special ingredients or oils, which can clog the plant's pores.

If you have very hard water or a water softener, you can use a spray bottle of distilled water to avoid harming your plant. I use this small spray bottle from Amazon and a clean washcloth. Spray each of the leaves, then gently wipe, and repeat until your plant is clean. You may need to clean each leaf two or three times.

Downsides of this method: Wiping the leaves can cause trauma to your plant, so this is my least favorite method. It's impossible to get the undersides of your plant's leaves clean, and this method is time-consuming. Finally, I find it cumbersome and messy, since the dirty spray water will drip down around your plant. You may want to put a towel beneath the plant to protect your floor.

◆ ◆ ◆

Take a look at your fiddle leaf fig plant's leaves to see whether it has gotten dusty or dirty over time. If it has, spring is the perfect time to clean your plant so that it can breathe easy and grow tall during the rest of the year.

SHOULD YOU USE LEAF SHINE PRODUCTS?

A clean, healthy fiddle leaf fig plant looks great and brings good energy to your home. There's no need to use additional leaf shine products on your plant. Oils and food products can clog the pores of your plant and cause infections, so never use milk, coconut oil, or cooking oils on your plant.

But if you do want shinier leaves and would like to use a commercial leaf shine product, be sure to purchase one made specifically for houseplants and not to overuse it. Follow the directions on the package, and be aware that some leaf shine products can attract more dust and require more regular cleanings.

"Plant roots so deeply in the people you love that you lose a piece of yourself when they go."

Pruning Your Fiddle Leaf Fig Plant

Given proper care, plenty of sunshine, and enough soil in which to expand its root ball, your fiddle leaf fig will grow quickly. Healthy plants may grow several inches or even a few feet each year. They can get lopsided or too big for their current location in a hurry. Pruning will keep your plant healthy, balanced, and a good size for its location. Below is your guide to properly pruning your fiddle leaf fig plant.

THE BENEFITS OF PRUNING

There are several reasons to prune your fiddle leaf fig plant. Pruning is essential for keeping it healthy and looking well—just like grooming your dog or cat. It also reduces unwanted growth.

REMOVE DAMAGED LEAVES AND STEMS

Regularly prune way damaged leaves and stems. Any leaves with large brown spots or holes can safely be removed to improve the overall health of your plant. An injured or sick leaf drains the resources of your plant and can spread an infection. When you notice damaged or sick leaves, remove them quickly any time of year.

KEEP YOUR PLANT FROM GETTING TOO TALL

Healthy fiddle leaf fig plants can grow aggressively toward the sun, which means they may get too large or too tall for their current location. Plants look best when their top leaves are at least eight to ten inches below the ceiling, so remove any growth above that height. By pruning your plant to keep it from getting too tall, you'll create a stronger and more compact plant.

GIVE YOUR PLANT SHAPE AND BALANCE

Grown indoors, fiddle leaf fig plants can take on unusual shapes because of their limited access to sunlight. Depending on where your plant is getting its light from, it may grow sideways toward the nearest window, which can leave your plant lopsided or off balance. To prevent this, it's important to rotate your plant at least once a month so that it grows symmetrically. Even then, plants may get off balance, and pruning will help keep growth from becoming lopsided.

In addition, when a fiddle leaf fig plant is growing in the wild, the lower leaves fall off due to lack of sunlight. But inside, lower leaves may still get plenty of light and remain on the plant. This can ruin the tree-like shape many people strive for. In order to shape your plant to look best for its location, you'll want to remove lower leaves and branches that are growing too wide.

DECREASE CROWDED AREAS

Fiddle leaf fig leaves need airflow and space to be healthy. If your plant gets too compact and crowded, the leaves can suffer damage from rubbing against each other. You'll want to thin crowded areas by pruning.

BEFORE YOU PRUNE

Try to prune your fiddle leaf fig in the spring or early summer. The best time is in the spring, when there is plenty of light to fuel recovery and new growth. You'll want to get a sharp pair of pruning shears, because dull tools or scissors can crush the stems and damage your plant.

Before you begin, be sure to put down an old sheet or a drop cloth, as each cut will bleed a sticky sap that can damage your floor and irritate skin. Next, clean and disinfect your tools, as germs on your tools can infect your plant. Run your shears through the dishwasher or thoroughly wash and dry with soap and water before you begin pruning.

PRUNING YOUR FIDDLE LEAF FIG

Shaping your fiddle leaf fig is a lot like sculpting a masterpiece. Have a vision of your end goal in mind before you begin. Be careful to think before you cut, because you cannot undo a severed branch. I find it's helpful to mark all of the branches I want to remove with colored tape or a Post-it Note before I start to make sure the leftover foliage looks balanced. Go slowly at first, and never remove more than ten percent of your plant at one time to reduce the risk of shock.

Assess the overall health of each branch and group of leaves so that you can plan to remove the least healthy areas of your plant first. If there are leaves with brown spots or branches with smaller leaf growth, mark those areas for removal.

If you have tightly crowded branches, you'll want to thin out some areas to provide improved airflow and reduce crowding. Any branches that touch should be addressed, as well as leaves that are impeding each other's growth.

Plan to remove any growth that is within eight to ten inches of the ceiling or surrounding walls and furniture. Then remove growth that does not fit within your ideal shape.

DECIDE ON YOUR IDEAL SHAPE

There are two general shapes of fiddle leaf fig plants. Smaller plants tend to be bushier, and larger plants tend to be more tree-shaped. As your small plant grows, you may want to begin to shape it into a tree. Decide whether you're trying to prune your plant towards a proper tree shape or keep it as a compact bush shape.

If you're going for a tree-like shape, you'll want to remove lower leaves and branches to reveal a proper trunk. If your plant is off-balance, you'll want to remove gangly or unsightly growth to create an attractive overall shape.

HOW TO MAKE YOUR CUTS

Once you've marked the areas you'd like to remove and verified that you are happy with the final shape, it's time to prune. Use sharp, clean shears to prune your plant and make sure the cutting motion is not crushing or damaging the stem.

Make each cut about half an inch from any leaves or the trunk. This allows your plant to properly heal without risk of infection to the main trunk or remaining leaves. Remove and dispose of any dropped leaves or debris to keep germs and infections from spreading.

NEW GROWTH AFTER PRUNING

Generally, if your plant is in good health, it will split a branch in two where it has been pruned. This eventually leads to the plant appearing fuller and healthier. However, if your plant is suffering or not getting enough light, it may continue to grow only one branch where it was cut. To encourage more growth, give access to plenty of light after pruning.

FERTILIZE AFTER PRUNING

To help your plant heal from the trauma of pruning and to encourage new growth, be sure to fertilize it regularly after pruning. You should see new growth within a couple of weeks to a month after pruning your plant.

◆ ◆ ◆

Pruning your plant gives you access to stem cuttings, so many people like to try to propagate their fiddle leaf fig at this time. If you are planning to use your pruned clippings for propagation, follow the steps in the next section to learn more.

"The creation of a thousand forests is in one acorn."

PROPAGATING
A FIDDLE LEAF
FIG PLANT

Propagating a plant involves taking a stem or leaf cutting and allowing it to root in water or soil to create a new self-sustaining plant. You can propagate most houseplants, with varying degrees of difficulty.

If you're a fiddle leaf fig aficionado trying to grow your herd, you may start to consider propagation so that you can grow many plants from one original. This saves money and allows you to clone your favorite fiddle leaf fig plant.

You may be intimidated by propagation, but fiddle leaf figs are actually relatively easy to propagate. You should be pruning your existing tree anyway, so why not try to root a few cuttings in water? It only takes four to six weeks for the roots to get started. If they don't take off, you can try again. Done right, propagating your plant gives you the ultimate joy: growing a brand-new plant of your very own from the beginning!

A word of caution, though. While propagating a fiddle leaf fig is possible, it may not be the best way to get a healthy new plant. A new plant grown from a cutting is not exactly the same as a commercially grown plant. The latter is most likely to have been grown from a process called "tissue culture," which produces stronger plants. Your time and money may be better spent cultivating a small commercially purchased fiddle leaf fig than propagating your own. However, if you'd still like to give propagation a try, follow the steps below to get started.

BEFORE YOU PROPAGATE YOUR FIDDLE LEAF FIG PLANT

The best time to propagate your plant is in the spring, when your plant is naturally growing and there's plenty of light available. But to ensure a successful outcome and a smooth process, there are a few things you'll want to do to prepare.

1. PLAN TO TRY AT LEAST THREE CUTTINGS

If you're putting in the time and energy to propagate your plant, it's wise to diversify your efforts. Try at least three cuttings so that if one or two aren't successful, you still have a backup plan. But don't take more than three cuttings from one plant unless it is very large, as you could shock it.

2. CHOOSE YOUR CONTAINERS

Use a separate clean container for each cutting so that if one cutting goes south, it won't affect the health of the others. Choose clear glass containers with wide mouths so that you can check the water level and your plant has some support. I recommend mason jars.

3. CONSIDER YOUR LOCATION

To give your cuttings the best environment for success, you'll need a bright place to put them for four to six weeks. Plenty of indirect light is best. Avoid direct sunlight, which will scorch your cuttings.

I chose this south-facing window, which is protected by a four-foot eave on the outside. The cuttings get bright light all day but no direct sun. You can see that a fiddle leaf fig and philodendron are already thriving here.

4. Strategize Your Cuttings

Which leaves should you cut? Should you take larger or smaller leaves? Should you take them from the top or the bottom of the plant? There are a few factors that will go into your decision on which leaves to cut.

First, look at your overall plant and take your cuttings from where you'd like to prune. For example, if you have a large branch you'd like to remove, you can take the cuttings from that branch without any part of the plant going to waste.

Another consideration is that smaller, younger leaves will do better. First, because they are smaller they have less nutrient and photosynthesis demands. Second, younger leaves are still actively growing, and so have higher concentrations of growth hormones. Choosing a newer leaf can give faster propagation results.

Finally, make sure to get a long enough stem to immerse in water. Even if you take only a leaf, you will need the leaf stem to be at least a half-inch long so that you can put the stem into water without submerging the leaf itself. In this first cutting, I don't have enough stem to give the leaf access to water without submerging the leaf itself, so it will probably fail. In this second cutting, a longer leaf stem allows the leaf to stay dry while the stem is fully immersed in water. It's critical to check the water level every few days to make sure the stem stays fully submerged.

5. Use a Clean, Sharp Tool

When you take a cutting, you need to get the cleanest cut possible and avoid crushing the stem during the cut. Use a clean, sharp tool such as pruning shears.

PROPAGATING A FIDDLE LEAF FIG PLANT IN SIX EASY STEPS

In this section, we'll review how to propagate in water. You can also propagate in soil, just be sure to keep the soil evenly moist as your new roots take hold.

Step One: Prepare Your Propagation Container

Have a container with clean, chlorine-free water or moist potting soil ready for your cutting. Allow normal tap water to sit overnight to let the chlorine evaporate or use distilled water. Make sure the container is a good size and shape to support your cutting and keep it upright.

Step Two: Take Your Stem Cutting

I recommend cutting a stem with two or three leaves (no more than this or they'll require too much energy to grow). Cut about three inches below the first leaf. This will give your new plant a short stem and enough leaves to sustain it. Choose the healthiest leaves on your plant to take for your cutting. Don't worry, they will grow back after you cut them. Use a clean, sharp tool to take your cutting and immediately place it into water.

Step Three: Use a Root Hormone

Purchase Fiddle Leaf Fig Propagation Root Hormone to help your plant grow new roots more quickly. Follow the

directions on the bottle and dip your stem in the root hormone once before placing it in water.

STEP FOUR: PLACE IN A BRIGHT LOCATION AND KEEP THE WATER CLEAN

Place your rooting system in a bright place without direct sunlight and check it every few days to make sure it has enough water and light. Replace the water with clean, chlorine-free water at room temperature if it looks dirty or cloudy.

Step Five: Wait One Month

It usually takes about one month for your cutting to develop roots. You will see the roots forming at the bottom of the plant after about four to six weeks. Allow them to grow for another week or so before you replant.

Step Six: Plant Your New Rooted Cutting

Plant your new rooted cutting in moist soil and be sure to keep it evenly moist for the first two months of growing to allow the roots to take hold. After three months, begin fertilizing regularly with Fiddle Leaf Fig Plant Food.

◆ ◆ ◆

It may take a year or so for your new plant to really get going, but with time, patience, and pruning, you'll have a brand-new fiddle leaf fig plant to enjoy. Propagation may seem technical or complex, but it's actually easy. And the joy of cultivating your own plant from a cutting exceeds any love you'll feel for a store-bought fiddle leaf fig plant!

PROPAGATING A FIDDLE LEAF FIG PLANT IN SIX EASY STEPS

Step One: Prepare Your Propagation Container.
Step Two: Take Your Stem Cutting.
Step Three: Use a Root Hormone.
Step Four: Place in a Bright Location and Keep the Water Clean.
Step Five: Wait One Month.
Step Six: Plant Your New Rooted Cutting.

"If you have a garden and a library, you have everything you need to be happy."

BONDING WITH
YOUR PLANT

It may sound strange, but research has repeatedly shown that plants grow better and are more resistant to disease when you form a relationship with them. Talking to your plants and playing music for them have been shown to help them thrive. New research by Michael Pollan, author of *The Botany of Desire*, even suggests that plants have intelligence and may be able to learn.

If you think about it, houseplants are perfect symbiotic partners for us. As we breathe out carbon dioxide, they clean our air and release perfect oxygen. They lower our stress levels, beautify our homes, and keep us company. We water them and keep them healthy. People who keep houseplants tend to live longer and enjoy better health.

Bonding with your plant may be the most important thing you do to ensure its longevity. Building a relationship with your fiddle leaf fig can help you identify when something is wrong, remember to water it on time, and enjoy your plant more. Don't be shy about spending time getting to know your plant better and forming a relationship with it.

Start by giving your plant a name and talking to it once in a while. Make it a point to check on your plant every week and appreciate new growth and good health. Finally, be thankful for the beautiful living creature in your home and enjoy your potentially lifelong relationship with your fiddle leaf fig plant!

"The best time to plant a tree was 25 years ago. The second best time is today."

IF YOU ENJOYED THIS BOOK, PLEASE LEAVE A REVIEW

I hope you enjoyed *The Fiddle Leaf Fig Expert*. If you did, please take a moment to leave a positive review on Amazon. It means the world to me! To learn more, go to fiddleleaffigplant.com or email me at claire@fiddleleaffigplant.com. Thanks for reading!

30501409R00060

Made in the USA
San Bernardino, CA
26 March 2019